EASY TEXAS COOKBOOK

AUTHENTIC SOUTHERN COOKING

By
Chef Maggie Chow
Copyright © 2015 by Saxonberg
Associates
All rights reserved

Published by
BookSumo, a division of Saxonberg
Associates
http://www.booksumo.com/

STAY TO THE END OF THE COOKBOOK AND RECEIVE....

I really appreciate when people, take the time to read all of my recipes.

So, as a gift for reading this entire cookbook you will receive a **massive collection of special recipes.**

Read to the end of and get my *Easy Specialty Cookbook Box Set for FREE*!

This box set includes the following:

1. ***Easy Sushi Cookbook***
2. ***Easy Dump Dinner Cookbook***
3. ***Easy Beans Cookbook***

Remember this box set is about **EASY** cooking.

In the ***Easy Sushi Cookbook*** you will learn the easiest methods to prepare almost every type of Japanese Sushi i.e. *California Rolls, the Perfect Sushi Rice, Crab Rolls, Osaka Style Sushi*, and so many others.

Then we go on to *Dump Dinners*. Nothing can be easier than a Dump Dinner. In the ***Easy Dump Dinner Cookbook*** we will learn how to master our slow cookers and make some amazingly unique dinners that will take almost ***no effort***.

Finally in the ***Easy Beans Cookbook*** we tackle one of my favorite side dishes: Beans. There are so many delicious ways to make Baked Beans and Bean Salads that I had to share them.

So stay till the end and then keep on cooking with my *Easy Specialty Cookbook Box Set*!

About the Author.

Maggie Chow is the author and creator of your favorite *Easy Cookbooks* and *The Effortless Chef Series*. Maggie is a lover of all things related to food. Maggie loves nothing more than finding new recipes, trying them out, and then making them her own, by adding or removing ingredients, tweaking cooking times, and anything to make the recipe not only taste better, but be easier to cook!

For a complete listing of all my books please see my author page.

INTRODUCTION

Welcome to *The Effortless Chef Series*! Thank you for taking the time to download the *Easy Texas Cookbook*. Come take a journey with me into the delights of easy cooking. The point of this cookbook and all my cookbooks is to exemplify the effortless nature of cooking simply.

In this book we focus on dishes from Texas. You will find that even though the recipes are simple, the taste of the dishes is quite amazing.

So will you join me in an adventure of simple cooking? If the answer is yes (and I hope it is) please consult the table of contents to find the dishes you are most interested in. Once you are ready jump right in and start cooking.

— Chef Maggie Chow

Table of Contents

Stay To the End of the Cookbook and Receive 2
About the Author 5
Introduction 7
Table of Contents 8
Any Issues? Contact Me 12
Legal Notes 13
Common Abbreviations 14
Chapter 1: Easy Texas Recipes 15
    Restaurant Style Lemon Tenderloins 15
    Authentic Texas Chili 18
    San Antonio Jambalaya 21
    Maggie's Easy Sheet Cake 24
    Southern Beef and Bean Salad 27
    Red White and Blue Patty 30
    Tex Mex Shrimp 33

Dallas Style Salsa 36
Texas Spareribs................................ 38
Real Southern Macaroni and Cheese 42
Texas Oven Roasted Squash............ 45
Pulled Pork 49
A Texan Dessert 52
(Sheet Cake)...................................... 52
Texas Brisket.................................... 55
Southern Gumbo I 58
Authentic Texas Burgers 62
Cajun Turkey Stew 65
A Southern Style Potato Salad......... 69
Easy Jalapeno Bites 72
Pinto Beans from Texas 75
Texas Style Fried Chicken 78
Sweet Honey Chicken...................... 82
Texas Mexican Burritos................... 85
Authentic Southern Corn 89
Black Eyed Peas in Texas 91
Classical Mexican Quesadillas I 94

Classical Mexican Quesadillas II 97
Texas Baked Beans 101
Mozzarella Chicken 104
Mexican Beef 107
Mexican Casserole 110
Rancho Minestrone Beef Soup 113
Maggie's Easy Texas Style Black Bean Burgers 116
(Vegetarian Approved) 116
Enchiladas 119
Mexican Style Rice 122
Cod Stew 124
Texas Casserole 127
Reuben 130
Texas Mexican Salad 133
A Texas Cajun Egg Sandwich Breakfast 136
Easy Texas Grilled Chicken 139
Hickory Mushroom Stuffed Burgers 142
Spicy Sweet Potatoes 145

Maggie's Favorite Armadillo Eggs . 148
Texas Mexican Shark with Noodles
.... 151
Texas Style Paella......................... 154
Cajun Fries.................................... 157
Texas Cayenne and Pepper Meatloaf
.... 160
Southern Linguine 164
Texas Style Spicy Rice 167
THANKS FOR READING! NOW LET'S TRY SOME **SUSHI** AND **DUMP DINNERS**....
.... 170
Come On... 172
Let's Be Friends :).......................... 172
Can I Ask A Favour? 173
Interested in Other Easy Cookbooks?
.... 174

Any Issues? Contact Me

If you find that something important to you is missing from this book please contact me at maggie@booksumo.com.

I will try my best to re-publish a revised copy taking your feedback into consideration and let you know when the book has been revised with you in mind.

:)

— Chef Maggie Chow

LEGAL NOTES

ALL RIGHTS RESERVED. NO PART OF THIS BOOK MAY BE REPRODUCED OR TRANSMITTED IN ANY FORM OR BY ANY MEANS. PHOTOCOPYING, POSTING ONLINE, AND / OR DIGITAL COPYING IS STRICTLY PROHIBITED UNLESS WRITTEN PERMISSION IS GRANTED BY THE BOOK'S PUBLISHING COMPANY. LIMITED USE OF THE BOOK'S TEXT IS PERMITTED FOR USE IN REVIEWS WRITTEN FOR THE PUBLIC AND/OR PUBLIC DOMAIN.

COMMON ABBREVIATIONS

cup(s)	C.
tablespoon	tbsp
teaspoon	tsp
ounce	oz.
pound	lb

*All units used are standard American measurements

Chapter 1: Easy Texas Recipes

Restaurant Style Lemon Tenderloins

Ingredients

- 1 tbsp butter
- 1/3 C. Italian salad dressing
- 1 lemon, zested and juiced
- 1 tbsp Worcestershire sauce
- 8 chicken tenderloins
- lemon pepper to taste
- garlic salt to taste
- onion powder to taste

Directions

- Add your butter to a casserole dish and place the dish in the oven. Now turn on the oven to

350 degrees before doing anything else.
- Let the butter melt as the oven warms. Once it is melted, remove the dish and add in: Worcestershire sauce, salad dressing, and lemon juice.
- Layer your pieces of chicken in the dish as well and cover them with the lemon sauce. Now top each side with: lemon zest, lemon pepper, onion powder, and garlic salt.
- Cook the chicken in the oven for 30 mins.
- Enjoy.

Amount per serving (4 total)

Timing Information:

Preparation	15 m
Cooking	25 m
Total Time	40 m

Nutritional Information:

Calories	214 kcal
Fat	11.2 g
Carbohydrates	6g
Protein	23.3 g
Cholesterol	70 mg
Sodium	581 mg

* Percent Daily Values are based on a 2,000 calorie diet.

Authentic Texas Chili

Ingredients

- 4 slices bacon, diced
- 2 onions, diced
- 8 cloves garlic, diced
- 2 tsps dried oregano
- 1 tsp cayenne pepper
- 3 tbsps paprika
- 1/3 C. chili powder
- 1 tbsp cumin
- 4 lbs boneless beef chuck or rump, cut into 1/2-inch cubes
- 5 3/4 C. water
- 4 canned Chipotle peppers in adobo sauce, seeded and minced
- 2 tbsps cornmeal

Directions

- Fry your bacon in a big pot then add in the garlic and onions. Cook the onions until they are

soft in the drippings then add in: cumin, oregano, chili powder, cayenne, and paprika.
- Cook the spice for 40 secs then add in: cornmeal, beef, chipotle, and water.
- Get everything boiling.
- Once the mix is boiling, reduce the heat, and cook everything for 3 hrs.
- At this point your stew should be thick and the beef should be soft.
- Enjoy.

Amount per serving (8 total)

Timing Information:

Preparation	20 m
Cooking	3 h
Total Time	3 h 20 m

Nutritional Information:

Calories	675 kcal
Fat	49.1 g
Carbohydrates	12.4g
Protein	42.4 g
Cholesterol	168 mg
Sodium	351 mg

* Percent Daily Values are based on a 2,000 calorie diet.

San Antonio Jambalaya

Ingredients

- 2 tbsps olive oil
- 1 C. diced onion
- 1/2 C. diced green bell pepper
- 1/2 C. diced celery
- 1 1/2 tsps diced garlic
- 1 C. converted long-grain white rice
- 4 oz. smoked sausage, cut into slices
- 4 oz. cooked ham, cut into bite-size pieces
- 2 (10 oz.) cans diced tomatoes with green chili peppers
- 1 C. chicken broth
- 1/4 tsp dried thyme
- 1 bay leaf
- 2 (15 oz.) cans ranch-style beans, undrained

Directions

- Stir fry the following until the onions are see through: onions, celery, and green peppers.
- Then add in the garlic and cook the mix for 2 more mins before adding the ham, sausage, and rice.
- Toast the rice for 4 mins then add the cans of tomatoes, broth, bay leaf, and thyme.
- Get everything boiling, place a lid on the pot, and cook the mix for 27 mins.
- Now add the beans and get everything hot.
- Enjoy.

Amount per serving (6 total)

Timing Information:

Preparation	10 m
Cooking	35 m
Total Time	45 m

Nutritional Information:

Calories	400 kcal
Fat	12.4 g
Carbohydrates	53.1g
Protein	17.3 g
Cholesterol	23 mg
Sodium	1541 mg

* Percent Daily Values are based on a 2,000 calorie diet.

Maggie's Easy Sheet Cake

Ingredients

- 1 C. butter
- 1 C. water
- 2 C. all-purpose flour
- 2 C. white sugar
- 2 eggs
- 1/2 C. sour cream
- 1 tsp almond extract
- 1/2 tsp salt
- 1 tsp baking soda
- 1/2 C. butter
- 1/4 C. milk
- 4 1/2 C. confectioners' sugar
- 1/2 tsp almond extract
- 1 C. diced walnuts

Directions

- Get a casserole dish, coat it with oil, and set your oven to 375

degrees before doing anything else.
- Boil your water and butter, then shut the heat, and add: baking soda, flour, salt, sugar, almond extract, eggs, and sour cream.
- Now add everything to the dish and cook the contents in the oven for 24 mins.
- Now get your milk and half a C. of butter boiling, shut the heat, and add in half a tsp of almond extract and sugar.
- Once the mix is smooth add the pecans.
- Top the cake with the sugar sauce.
- Enjoy.

Amount per serving (24 total)

Timing Information:

Preparation	10 m
Cooking	40 m
Total Time	1 h

Nutritional Information:

Calories	342 kcal
Fat	16.3 g
Carbohydrates	48.1g
Protein	2.7 g
Cholesterol	48 mg
Sodium	193 mg

* Percent Daily Values are based on a 2,000 calorie diet.

Southern Beef and Bean Salad

Ingredients

- 1 lb lean ground beef
- 2 tbsps chili powder
- 1/2 tsp ground cumin
- salt and pepper to taste
- 1 head iceberg lettuce, shredded
- 1 (15.5 oz.) can pinto beans
- 2 tomatoes, cubed
- 1 C. shredded Cheddar cheese
- 1/4 C. diced fresh cilantro
- 1 (12 oz.) package corn tortilla chips, broken
- 1 jalapeno pepper, seeded and diced (optional)
- 1/2 C. diced green onion (optional)
- 1 C. salsa (optional)

Directions

- Fry your beef until fully done then add in: pepper, chili powder, salt, and cumin.
- Get a bowl, combine: pinto beans with liquid, jalapenos, lettuce, salsa, cilantro, onions, tomatoes, and cheddar.
- Now add the corn chips and stir before adding the beef and mixing one more time.
- Enjoy.

Amount per serving (6 total)

Timing Information:

Preparation	15 m
Cooking	10 m
Total Time	25 m

Nutritional Information:

Calories	674 kcal
Fat	37.7 g
Carbohydrates	57.5 g
Protein	29.5 g
Cholesterol	81 mg
Sodium	1043 mg

* Percent Daily Values are based on a 2,000 calorie diet.

Red White and Blue Patty

Ingredients

- 1 lb ground beef
- 3 tbsps chili seasoning mix
- 2 chipotle peppers in adobo sauce, minced
- 1/4 C. mayonnaise
- 1 chipotle pepper in adobo sauce, minced
- 6 (1 oz.) slices white bread
- 6 (1/2 oz.) slices pepperjack cheese

Directions

- Get a bowl, combine: adobo sauce, ground beef, 2 chipotle peppers, and chili seasoning.
- Now, with your hands, form three burgers from the mix.
- Get a 2nd bowl, combine: 1 chipotle pepper and the mayo.

- Coat your pieces of bread with this mix, and add a piece of cheese.
- Now fry your burgers for 6 mins per side then place them on top of the cheese.
- Place another piece of bread to from a burger.
- Remove some of the drippings from the pan and, for 2 mins, fry each side of the burger in the hot drippings.
- Enjoy.

Amount per serving (3 total)

Timing Information:

Preparation	15 m
Cooking	10 m
Total Time	25 m

Nutritional Information:

Calories	691 kcal
Fat	44.2 g
Carbohydrates	35.4g
Protein	37.3 g
Cholesterol	129 mg
Sodium	1574 mg

* Percent Daily Values are based on a 2,000 calorie diet.

Tex Mex Shrimp

Ingredients

- 1 lb cooked medium shrimp, chilled
- 1/2 large cucumber, cut into 1/2 inch cubes
- 1/2 large tomato, cut into 1/2 inch cubes
- 8 green onions, thinly sliced
- 1 oz. fresh cilantro, finely diced
- 1 serrano pepper, thinly sliced
- 1 (8 oz.) can tomato sauce
- 2 tbsps white vinegar
- 1 lime

Directions

- Get a bowl, combine: vinegar, shrimp, tomato sauce, cucumber, serrano, green onions, and cilantro.

- Top this mix with the lime and place it in the fridge until chilled.
- Enjoy.

Amount per serving (8 total)

Timing Information:

Preparation	
Cooking	20 m
Total Time	20 m

Nutritional Information:

Calories	76 kcal
Fat	0.8 g
Carbohydrates	4.8g
Protein	12.9 g
Cholesterol	111 mg
Sodium	279 mg

* Percent Daily Values are based on a 2,000 calorie diet.

Dallas Style Salsa

Ingredients

- 3 tbsps diced fresh chives
- 1/2 bunch fresh cilantro
- 2 cloves garlic, diced
- 2 (14 oz.) cans stewed tomatoes
- 2 serrano chilis, seeded and diced
- salt and pepper to taste

Directions

- Pulse the following in a blender: pepper, chives, salt, cilantro, tomatoes, and garlic.
- Serve the mix over cooked white rice.
- Enjoy.

Amount per serving (12 total)

Timing Information:

Preparation	
Cooking	5 m
Total Time	5 m

Nutritional Information:

Calories	21 kcal
Fat	0.2 g
Carbohydrates	< 5g
Protein	0.8 g
Cholesterol	0 mg
Sodium	146 mg

* Percent Daily Values are based on a 2,000 calorie diet.

Texas Spareribs

Ingredients

- 6 lbs pork spareribs, rinsed, and fat removed
- 1 1/2 C. white sugar
- 1/4 C. salt
- 2 1/2 tbsps ground black pepper
- 3 tbsps sweet paprika
- 1 tsp cayenne pepper, or to taste
- 2 tbsps garlic powder
- 5 tbsps pan drippings
- 1/2 C. diced onion
- 4 C. ketchup
- 3 C. hot water
- 4 tbsps brown sugar
- cayenne pepper to taste
- salt and pepper to taste
- 1 C. wood chips, soaked

Directions

- Get a bowl, combine: garlic powder, sugar, 1 tsp cayenne, 1/4 C. salt, paprika, and black pepper.
- Cover your ribs with this dry rub.
- Now take two casserole dishes and divide the ribs between them.
- Place some plastic wrap around the dishes and chill the contents in the fridge overnight.
- Now set your oven to 275 degrees before doing anything else.
- Cook the ribs for 4 hrs in the oven.
- Take about 6 tbsps of rendered fat from the roasting, add it to a pot, and begin to stir fry your onions in it, until they are soft.
- Now add the ketchup and cook everything for 5 mins.
- Add in: pepper, water, salt, brown sugar, and cayenne.
- Get everything boiling, place a lid on the pot, set the heat to a low level, and gently cook the mix for 60 mins.

- Now get your grill hot and oil the grate.
- Grill 2 racks of ribs for 25 mins at a time.
- Then continue grilling the remaining meat.
- When the ribs are done top them with the brown sugar coating.
- Enjoy.

Timing Information:

Preparation	30 m
Cooking	5 h
Total Time	13 h 30 m

Nutritional Information:

Calories	30.9 g
Fat	53.1g
Carbohydrates	33.4 g
Protein	127 mg
Cholesterol	3316 mg
Sodium	30.9 g

* Percent Daily Values are based on a 2,000 calorie diet.

Real Southern Macaroni and Cheese

Ingredients

- 2 tbsps butter
- 1/4 C. finely diced onion
- 2 tbsps all-purpose flour
- 2 C. milk
- 3/4 tsp salt
- 1/2 tsp dry mustard
- 1/4 tsp ground black pepper
- 1 (8 oz.) package elbow macaroni
- 2 C. shredded sharp Cheddar cheese
- 1 (8 oz.) package processed American cheese, cut into strips

Directions

- Set your oven to 350 degrees before doing anything else.

- Boil your pasta for 9 mins in water and salt. Then remove all the liquids.
- Stir fry your onions in butter for 4 mins then add the flour and cook the mix for 20 more secs while mixing.
- Now add in: pepper, milk, mustard, and salt.
- Continue to heat and stir, until everything starts boiling and becomes thick.
- Once the sauce has become thick add in the cheese and cook the sauce until the cheese melts, while continuing to stir.
- Add the pasta to the sauce, stir the mix once, and then pour everything into a casserole dish.
- Cook the contents in the oven for 35 mins.
- Enjoy.

Amount per serving (6 total)

Timing Information:

Preparation	10 m
Cooking	45 m
Total Time	1 h 5 m

Nutritional Information:

Calories	561 kcal
Fat	33.3 g
Carbohydrates	36.5g
Protein	28.3 g
Cholesterol	100 mg
Sodium	1194 mg

* Percent Daily Values are based on a 2,000 calorie diet.

Texas Oven Roasted Squash

Ingredients

- 1 lb ground beef
- 1/4 C. olive oil, divided
- 4 zucchini, cut into 1/2-inch cubes
- 1 red bell pepper, diced
- 1 jalapeno pepper, seeded and diced
- 4 cloves garlic, minced
- 4 green onions, diced -- white and green parts separated
- salt and pepper to taste
- 3 tbsps tomato paste
- 4 tsps chili powder, or to taste
- 2 tsps ground cumin, or to taste
- 1 (15 oz.) can black beans, rinsed and drained
- 1 (15 oz.) can kidney beans, rinsed and drained
- 1 C. frozen corn, thawed
- 1/2 C. grated Parmesan cheese, divided

- 1/4 C. diced fresh cilantro

Directions

- Stir fry your beef until fully done, for 10 mins, then break it into pieces.
- Now remove the meat from the pan.
- Coat a casserole dish with 1 tsp of olive oil and then set your oven to 400 degrees before doing anything else.
- Now add the rest of the oil to a pan and stir fry the following for 5 mins: green onions, zucchini, garlic, bell peppers, and jalapenos.
- Top the veggies with some pepper and salt. Then add: cumin, tomato paste, and chili powder.
- Let the contents gently boil for 60 secs then shut the heat.
- Add to the mix: a quarter of a C. of parmesan, ground beef, corn, kidney beans, and black beans.

- Pour the contents into the casserole dish and top everything with the rest of the parmesan.
- Place a covering of foil on the dish and cook everything in the oven for 27 mins.
- Now take off the foil and continue cooking for 5 more mins.
- Before serving, add a topping of cilantro.
- Enjoy.

Amount per serving (8 total)

Timing Information:

Preparation	30 m
Cooking	40 m
Total Time	1 h 10 m

Nutritional Information:

Calories	281 kcal
Fat	15.8 g
Carbohydrates	20g
Protein	17 g
Cholesterol	39 mg
Sodium	298 mg

* Percent Daily Values are based on a 2,000 calorie diet.

Pulled Pork

Ingredients

- 1 tsp vegetable oil
- 1 (4 lb) pork shoulder roast
- 1 C. barbeque sauce
- 1/2 C. apple cider vinegar
- 1/2 C. chicken broth
- 1/4 C. light brown sugar
- 1 tbsp prepared yellow mustard
- 1 tbsp Worcestershire sauce
- 1 tbsp chili powder
- 1 extra large onion, diced
- 2 large cloves garlic, crushed
- 1 1/2 tsps dried thyme
- 8 hamburger buns, split
- 2 tbsps butter, or as needed

Directions

- Get a bowl, combine pork and veggie oil. Then place everything the crock pot.

- Now add: thyme, bbq sauce, garlic, vinegar, onions, broth, chili powder, brown sugar, Worcestershire, and yellow mustard.
- Stir the contents and cook the mix for 6 hrs with high heat.
- Now take out the pork and shred it before placing everything back into the pot and stirring.
- Coat your buns with butter and fry them for 1 min in a pan with the buttery side facing downwards.
- Now liberally top the pieces of bread with the shredded pork and sauce.
- Enjoy.

Amount per serving (8 total)

Timing Information:

Preparation	15 m
Cooking	5 h
Total Time	5 h 15 m

Nutritional Information:

Calories	527 kcal
Fat	23.1 g
Carbohydrates	45.5g
Protein	31.9 g
Cholesterol	98 mg
Sodium	790 mg

* Percent Daily Values are based on a 2,000 calorie diet.

A Texan Dessert

(Sheet Cake)

Ingredients

- 2 C. all-purpose flour
- 2 C. white sugar
- 1 tsp baking soda
- 1/2 tsp salt
- 1/2 C. sour cream
- 2 eggs
- 1 C. butter
- 1 C. water
- 5 tbsps unsweetened cocoa powder
- 6 tbsps milk
- 5 tbsps unsweetened cocoa powder
- 1/2 C. butter
- 4 C. confectioners' sugar
- 1 tsp vanilla extract
- 1 C. diced walnuts (optional)

Directions

- Coat a casserole dish with oil and flour.
- Now set your oven to 350 degrees before doing anything else.
- Get a bowl, mix: eggs, flour, sour cream, sugar, salt, and baking soda.
- Combine the cocoa powder with the butter and water in a pan.
- Heat and stir the mix until smooth and boiling.
- Then add it with the sour cream mix and combine both mixes.
- Add this batter to the dish and cook it for 22 mins in the oven.
- At the same time get the following boiling: half a C. of butter, milk, and 5 tbsps of cocoa.
- Once the mixing is boiling combine in the vanilla and confectioner's.
- Now add the walnuts, and top the cake with this mix.
- Enjoy.

Amount per serving (32 total)

Timing Information:

Preparation	10 m
Cooking	20 m
Total Time	30 m

Nutritional Information:

Calories	256 kcal
Fat	12.5 g
Carbohydrates	35.8g
Protein	2.4 g
Cholesterol	36 mg
Sodium	145 mg

* Percent Daily Values are based on a 2,000 calorie diet.

Texas Brisket

Ingredients

- 4 lbs lean beef brisket
- 2 tbsps liquid smoke flavoring
- 1 tbsp onion salt
- 1 tbsp garlic salt
- 1 1/2 tbsps brown sugar
- 1 C. ketchup
- 3 tbsps butter
- 1/4 C. water
- 1/2 tsp celery salt
- 1 tbsp liquid smoke flavoring
- 2 tbsps Worcestershire sauce
- 1 1/2 tsps mustard powder
- salt and pepper to taste

Directions

- Coat your beef with liquid smoke and then top it with garlic and onion salt.

- Wrap everything with some foil and place it in the fridge for 8 hours.
- Now set your oven to 300 degrees before doing anything else.
- Place the beef in a roasting dish and place a covering of foil around it.
- Cook the beef in the oven for 6 hrs. Then when it is cool slice it into pieces.
- Now get the following boiling: pepper, brown sugar, salt, ketchup, mustard, butter, Worcestershire, water, liquid smoke, and celery.
- Let the mix thicken and then top your beef with it and cook the meat in the oven for 65 more mins.
- Enjoy.

Amount per serving (10 total)

Timing Information:

Preparation	10 m
Cooking	6 h
Total Time	14 h 10 m

Nutritional Information:

Calories	560 kcal
Fat	42.3 g
Carbohydrates	9.3g
Protein	34.1 g
Cholesterol	133 mg
Sodium	1613 mg

* Percent Daily Values are based on a 2,000 calorie diet.

Southern Gumbo I

Ingredients

- 1 (3 lb) whole chicken
- 1/2 C. all-purpose flour
- 1/2 C. vegetable oil
- 1 (10 oz.) package frozen chopped onions
- 1 (10 oz.) package frozen green bell peppers
- 5 stalks celery, finely chopped
- 1 tbsp Cajun seasoning (such as Tony Chachere's), or to taste
- 2 whole bay leaves
- 1 (28 oz.) can diced tomatoes
- 1 lb fully-cooked smoked beef sausage (such as Hillshire Farm(R)), sliced
- 1 (10 oz.) package frozen sliced okra
- salt and black pepper to taste

Directions

- Boil your water and salt, then simmer your chicken in it for 1 hour until fully cooked.
- Take the chicken out from the water and cut it in half to cool faster.
- Keep the water the chicken was cooked in.
- Once the chicken is no longer hot take off the meat from the bones.
- Now get a big pan and mix: veggie oil and flour together to form a roux.
- Make this roux with a low level of heat and constantly stir it for about 22 mins until it becomes brown.
- Once it is brown add in: bay leaves, onions, Cajun seasoning, celery and bell peppers.
- Again with a low heat let the veggies simmer for 40 mins.
- Now add the chicken broth (the boiled water), sausage, and diced tomatoes.
- Let the contents simmer for 1 more hour.

- Now add in your meat from the chicken and your okra and let everything simmer for 50 more mins.
- Enjoy your gumbo.

Amount per serving (10 total)

Timing Information:

Preparation	20 m
Cooking	3 h 15 m
Total Time	3 h 55 m

Nutritional Information:

Calories	437 kcal
Fat	32.2 g
Carbohydrates	14.5g
Protein	21.4 g
Cholesterol	67 mg
Sodium	873 mg

* Percent Daily Values are based on a 2,000 calorie diet.

Authentic Texas Burgers

Ingredients

- 1/2 C. mayonnaise
- 1 tsp Cajun seasoning
- 1 1/3 lbs ground beef sirloin
- 1 jalapeno pepper, seeded and diced
- 1/2 C. diced white onion
- 1 clove garlic, minced
- 1 tbsp Cajun seasoning
- 1 tsp Worcestershire sauce
- 4 slices pepperjack cheese
- 4 hamburger buns, split
- 4 leaves lettuce
- 4 slices tomato

Directions

- Get your grill hot and oil the grate.
- Get a bowl, combine: 1 tbsp of Cajun spice and mayo.

- Get a 2nd bowl, combine: Worcestershire, beef, 1 tbsp Cajun spice, jalapenos, garlic, and onions.
- Now shape the beef mix into 4 burgers.
- Grill the burgers for 6 mins each side.
- Place a piece of cheese on each patty on the grill and heat them until the cheese melts.
- Coat your buns with the Cajun mayo, a beef patty, a piece of tomato, and some lettuce.
- Enjoy.

Amount per serving (4 total)

Timing Information:

Preparation	25 m
Cooking	15 m
Total Time	40 m

Nutritional Information:

Calories	714 kcal
Fat	49.1 g
Carbohydrates	28.5g
Protein	38.3 g
Cholesterol	132 mg
Sodium	1140 mg

* Percent Daily Values are based on a 2,000 calorie diet.

Cajun Turkey Stew

Ingredients

- 1 tbsp olive oil
- 1/2 C. minced onion
- 3 cloves garlic, minced
- 2 tsps chili powder
- 1/2 tsp cumin
- 1/2 tsp oregano
- 4 C. water
- 1 (10.75 oz.) can condensed tomato soup
- 1 (28 oz.) can diced tomatoes
- 1 C. salsa
- 4 C. shredded cooked turkey
- 1 tbsp dried parsley
- 3 chicken bouillon cubes
- 1 (14 oz.) can black beans, rinsed, drained
- 2 C. frozen corn
- 1/2 C. sour cream
- 1/4 C. diced fresh cilantro
- Toppings:
- 6 C. corn tortilla chips

- 3/4 C. diced green onion
- 1 C. shredded Cheddar-Monterey Jack cheese blend
- 1/2 C. diced fresh cilantro
- 1/2 C. sour cream

Directions

- Stir fry your onions in olive oil for 5 mins then combine in: oregano, garlic, cumin, and chili powder.
- Cook the spices for 60 more secs.
- Now add the following and get it boiling: bouillon, water, parsley, tomato soup, turkey, diced tomatoes, and salsa.
- Once the bouillon has been combined into the mix add: cilantro, black beans, sour cream, and corn.
- Let the mix gently cook for 33 mins with a low level of heat.
- When serving the soup top the bowl with shredded cheese, tortilla chips, green onions, cilantro, and more sour cream.

- Enjoy.

Amount per serving (6 total)

Timing Information:

Preparation	10 m
Cooking	40 m
Total Time	50 m

Nutritional Information:

Calories	684 kcal
Fat	30.5 g
Carbohydrates	59.2g
Protein	45.7 g
Cholesterol	112 mg
Sodium	2036 mg

* Percent Daily Values are based on a 2,000 calorie diet.

A Southern Style Potato Salad

Ingredients

- 1 (1 oz.) package ranch dressing mix
- 2 C. mayonnaise
- 3/4 C. diced green onion
- 1 lb bacon slices
- 5 lbs unpeeled red potatoes

Directions

- For 22 mins boil your potatoes in water and salt. Then remove the liquid and chunk the potatoes when cool.
- Place the chunks in a bowl and chill them in the fridge for 3 hrs.
- Get a 2nd bowl, combine: green onions, mayo, and ranch.

- Place a covering of plastic on this bowl, and place it in the fridge as well for 3 hours.
- For 17 mins microwave your bacon wrapped in paper towels.
- Once the bacon is cool, break it into pieces.
- Add the bacon to the mayo mix.
- Stir everything then add the mayo mix to the bowl with the potatoes.
- Stir everything again, then serve.
- Enjoy.

Amount per serving (16 total)

Timing Information:

Preparation	30 m
Cooking	30 m
Total Time	1 h

Nutritional Information:

Calories	353 kcal
Fat	25.9 g
Carbohydrates	24.8g
Protein	6.5 g
Cholesterol	21 mg
Sodium	503 mg

* Percent Daily Values are based on a 2,000 calorie diet.

Easy Jalapeno Bites

Ingredients

- 2 (12 oz.) packages ground sausage
- 2 (8 oz.) packages cream cheese, softened
- 30 jalapeno chili peppers, cut in half horizontally, seeds taken out
- 1 lb sliced bacon, cut in half

Directions

- Set your oven to 375 degrees before doing anything else.
- Stir fry your sausage until fully done then place them in a bowl with the cream cheese.
- Fill your pieces of pepper with the sausage mix and then wrap bacon around each one.
- Place the contents into a casserole dish and cook

everything in the oven for 24 mins.
- Enjoy.

Amount per serving (20 total)

Timing Information:

Preparation	1 h
Cooking	20 m
Total Time	1 h 20 m

Nutritional Information:

Calories	189 kcal
Fat	18.2 g
Carbohydrates	2g
Protein	< 4.6 g
Cholesterol	40 mg
Sodium	256 mg

* Percent Daily Values are based on a 2,000 calorie diet.

Pinto Beans from Texas

Ingredients

- 1 lb dry pinto beans
- 1 (29 oz.) can reduced sodium chicken broth
- 1 large onion, diced
- 1 fresh jalapeno pepper, diced
- 2 cloves garlic, minced
- 1/2 C. green salsa
- 1 tsp cumin
- 1/2 tsp ground black pepper
- water, if needed

Directions

- Get the following boiling: pepper, beans, cumin, broth, onions, salsa, jalapenos, and garlic.
- Let the contents cook for 2 hrs.
- If the mix gets too dry add some water and continue cooking for the remaining time.

- Enjoy.

Amount per serving (8 total)

Timing Information:

Preparation	15 m
Cooking	2 h
Total Time	2 h 15 m

Nutritional Information:

Calories	210 kcal
Fat	1.1 g
Carbohydrates	37.9g
Protein	13.2 g
Cholesterol	1 mg
Sodium	< 95 mg

* Percent Daily Values are based on a 2,000 calorie diet.

Texas Style Fried Chicken

Ingredients

- 2 C. buttermilk
- 1 tsp onion powder
- 1/4 C. diced fresh parsley
- 1/4 C. diced fresh tarragon
- 1/4 C. diced fresh sage
- 1 tsp paprika
- 1 tsp ground cayenne pepper
- 2 skinless, boneless chicken breast halves, halved
- 2 C. all-purpose flour
- 1 tsp garlic salt
- 1 tsp onion salt
- 1 tsp ground cayenne pepper
- salt and ground black pepper to taste
- 2 eggs
- 2 tbsps whole milk
- ground black pepper to taste
- 2 C. grapeseed oil for frying
- 1/2 C. all-purpose flour

- 1/2 C. quick-mixing flour (such as Wondra(R))
- 2 C. whole milk
- 1 pinch salt and ground white pepper to taste

Directions

- Get a bowl, combine: 1 tsp cayenne, buttermilk, paprika, onion powder, sage, parsley, and tarragon.
- Add in your chicken to the mix and coat the pieces evenly.
- Place a covering of plastic on the bowl and put everything in the fridge overnight.
- Get a 2nd bowl, mix: black pepper, 2 C. flour, salt, garlic salt, 1 tsp cayenne, and onion salt.
- Get a 3rd bowl, whisk: 2 tbsps milk, eggs, pepper, and salt.
- Get a 4rd bowl and add in 1/2 C. of flour without any spices.

- Dredge your chicken first in the 4th bowl, then the 3rd bowl, and finally the 2nd.
- For 10 mins, per side, fry your chicken in grapeseed oil then place on a rack.
- Leave a quarter of a C. of oil in the pan and begin adding the quick mix flour and milk to the oil while stirring.
- Get the mixing gently boiling and continue stirring until the gravy is thick.
- Now add some pepper and salt and top the chicken pieces with it.
- Enjoy.

Amount per serving (4 total)

Timing Information:

Preparation	30 m
Cooking	20 m
Total Time	8 h 50 m

Nutritional Information:

Calories	666 kcal
Fat	21.3 g
Carbohydrates	85.6g
Protein	32.7 g
Cholesterol	140 mg
Sodium	1151 mg

* Percent Daily Values are based on a 2,000 calorie diet.

Sweet Honey Chicken

Ingredients

- 3 C. cold water
- 1/4 C. kosher salt
- 1/4 C. honey
- 4 boneless skinless chicken breast halves
- 1/4 C. buttermilk
- 1 C. all-purpose flour
- 1 tsp black pepper
- 1/2 tsp garlic salt
- 1/2 tsp onion salt
- cayenne pepper to taste
- vegetable oil for frying

Directions

- Get a bowl, combine: honey, water, and salt.
- Now place the chicken in the water (make sure the liquid covers the chicken).

- Place a covering of plastic wrap around the bowl and chill the mix in the fridge for 2 hrs.
- Now put your chicken in another bowl and cover it with buttermilk.
- Let the chicken stand for 30 mins in the milk.
- Add your veggie oil to a frying and pan and begin heating it to 350 degrees before doing anything else.
- Now get a 3rd bowl, mix: cayenne, flour, onion salt, garlic salt, and black pepper.
- Dredge your chicken in the dry mix then fry it for 13 mins per side in the hot oil
- Enjoy.

Amount per serving (4 total)

Timing Information:

Preparation	10 m
Cooking	15 m
Total Time	1 h 45 m

Nutritional Information:

Calories	481 kcal
Fat	21.5 g
Carbohydrates	49.4g
Protein	22.8 g
Cholesterol	65 mg
Sodium	6378 mg

* Percent Daily Values are based on a 2,000 calorie diet.

Texas Mexican Burritos

Ingredients

- 1 lb ground beef
- 1/2 C. diced onion
- 1 clove garlic, minced
- 1/2 tsp cumin
- 1/4 tsp salt
- 1/8 tsp pepper
- 1 (4.5 oz.) can diced green chili peppers
- 1 (16 oz.) can refried beans
- 1 (15 oz.) can chili without beans
- 1 (10.75 oz.) can condensed tomato soup
- 1 (10 oz.) can enchilada sauce
- 6 (12 inch) flour tortillas, warmed
- 2 C. shredded lettuce
- 1 C. diced tomatoes
- 2 C. shredded Mexican blend cheese
- 1/2 C. diced green onions

Directions

- Stir fry and crumble your beef in a frying pan until it is fully done.
- Then add in the onions and continue frying the onions until they are see-through.
- Remove the excess oil and add: pepper, beans, garlic, green chilies, salt, and cumin.
- Get all the contents hot and then shut the heat.
- Now in another big pot heat the following: enchilada sauce, chili without beans, and tomato soup.
- Add half a C. of beef to a tortilla, and add some tomato and lettuce.
- Form an enchilada by rolling the tortilla.
- Now add a liberal amount of tomato mix over the enchilada and a topping of green onions and cheese.
- For 40 secs heat the enchilada in the microwave.
- Continue for the rest of the ingredients.

- Enjoy.

Amount per serving (6 total)

Timing Information:

Preparation	15 m
Cooking	30 m
Total Time	45 m

Nutritional Information:

Calories	916 kcal
Fat	42 g
Carbohydrates	92g
Protein	43.9 g
Cholesterol	122 mg
Sodium	2285 mg

* Percent Daily Values are based on a 2,000 calorie diet.

Authentic Southern Corn

Ingredients

- 2 (15.25 oz.) cans whole kernel corn, drained
- 1 (8 oz.) package cream cheese
- 1/4 C. butter
- 10 jalapeno peppers, diced
- 1 tsp garlic salt

Directions

- Cook the following for 15 mins, in a large, pot: garlic salt, corn, jalapenos, butter, and cream cheese.
- Stir the mix every 2 to 3 mins.
- Enjoy.

Amount per serving (6 total)

Timing Information:

Preparation	10 m
Cooking	10 m
Total Time	20 m

Nutritional Information:

Calories	359 kcal
Fat	22.7 g
Carbohydrates	38.2g
Protein	8 g
Cholesterol	61 mg
Sodium	491 mg

* Percent Daily Values are based on a 2,000 calorie diet.

Black Eyed Peas in Texas

Ingredients

- 1/2 onion, diced
- 1 green bell pepper, diced
- 1 bunch green onions, diced
- 2 jalapeno peppers, diced
- 1 tbsp minced garlic
- 1 pint cherry tomatoes, quartered
- 1 (8 oz.) bottle zesty Italian dressing
- 1 (15 oz.) can black beans, drained
- 1 (15 oz.) can black-eyed peas, drained
- 1/2 tsp ground coriander
- 1 bunch diced fresh cilantro

Directions

- Get a bowl, combine: coriander, onions, black eyed peas, bell peppers, dressing, garlic, and cherry tomatoes.

- Place a covering of plastic over the bowl, and place everything in the fridge for 4 hrs.
- Now add a topping of fresh cilantro.
- Enjoy.

Amount per serving (16 total)

Timing Information:

Preparation	
Cooking	15 m
Total Time	1 h 15 m

Nutritional Information:

Calories	107 kcal
Fat	5.4 g
Carbohydrates	11.8g
Protein	3.5 g
Cholesterol	0 mg
Sodium	415 mg

* Percent Daily Values are based on a 2,000 calorie diet.

Classical Mexican Quesadillas I

Ingredients

- 2 tbsps vegetable oil, divided
- 1 onion, sliced into rings
- 1 tbsp honey
- 2 skinless, boneless chicken breast halves - cut into strips
- 1/2 C. barbeque sauce
- 1/2 C. shredded sharp Cheddar cheese
- 1/2 C. shredded Monterey Jack cheese
- 8 (10 inch) flour tortillas

Directions

- Set your oven to 350 degrees before doing anything else.
- Stir fry your onions in oil for 7 mins then place them to the side.

- Add in some more oil and begin to cook your chicken in it until it is fully done.
- Pour in the bbq sauce and make sure the chicken is covered.
- Equally divide the following ingredients between your tortillas: Monterey, chicken, cheddar, and onions.
- Then place another tortilla on top.
- In batches of two cook the quesadillas in the oven for 25 mins.
- Slice each one into 4 pieces.
- Enjoy.

Amount per serving (8 total)

Timing Information:

Preparation	20 m
Cooking	15 m
Total Time	35 m

Nutritional Information:

Calories	411 kcal
Fat	14.3 g
Carbohydrates	46.2g
Protein	23.2 g
Cholesterol	48 mg
Sodium	753 mg

* Percent Daily Values are based on a 2,000 calorie diet.

Classical Mexican Quesadillas II

Ingredients

- 2 tomatoes, diced
- 1 onion, finely diced
- 2 limes, juiced
- 2 tbsps diced fresh cilantro
- 1 jalapeno pepper, seeded and minced
- salt and pepper to taste
- 2 tbsps olive oil, divided
- 2 skinless, boneless chicken breast halves - cut into strips
- 1/2 onion, thinly sliced
- 1 green bell pepper, thinly sliced
- 2 cloves garlic, minced
- 4 (12 inch) flour tortillas
- 1 C. shredded Monterey Jack cheese
- 1/4 C. sour cream, for topping

Directions

- Get a bowl, combine: pepper, tomatoes, salt, onions, jalapenos, cilantro, and lime juice.
- This is your Pico de Gallo.
- Now stir fry your chicken in olive oil until fully done and place it to the side.
- Add in a bit more olive oil and being to stir fry your sliced onions and green pepper until soft, then add the garlic and cook everything for 1 more min.
- Add in half of the tomato mix and the chicken.
- Get the contents hot.
- Now shut the heat.
- Get a 2nd pan and layer the following in it: 1 tortilla, a quarter of a C. of cheese, half of the chicken mix, and another quarter of a C. of cheese.
- Now layer an additional tortilla.
- Brown one side of the quesadilla and then turn it over.

- Brown the opposite side of the quesadilla and cut it into 4 pieces.
- Now continue the process for the rest of the ingredients.
- Top each quesadilla piece with a dollop of sour cream and more tomato mix.
- Enjoy.

Amount per serving (4 total)

Timing Information:

Preparation	25 m
Cooking	30 m
Total Time	55 m

Nutritional Information:

Calories	673 kcal
Fat	29.1 g
Carbohydrates	72.8g
Protein	31 g
Cholesterol	65 mg
Sodium	940 mg

* Percent Daily Values are based on a 2,000 calorie diet.

Texas Baked Beans

Ingredients

- 1 (28 oz.) can baked beans with pork
- 1 medium onion, diced
- 1 medium bell pepper, diced
- 4 links spicy pork sausage, cut into chunks
- 2 tbsps chili powder
- 3 tbsps Worcestershire sauce
- 4 tbsps vinegar
- 1/2 C. packed brown sugar
- 1/2 C. ketchup
- 1 tsp garlic powder
- salt to taste
- 1 dash cayenne pepper (optional)

Directions

- Set your oven to 350 degrees before doing anything else.

- Add the following to a Dutch oven: sausage, salt, beans, garlic powder, onions, ketchup, bell peppers, brown sugar, chili powder, cayenne, vinegar, and Worcestershire sauce.
- Place the lid on the pot and the place everything in the oven for 65 mins.
- Enjoy.

Amount per serving (6 total)

Timing Information:

Preparation	15 m
Cooking	1 h
Total Time	1 h 15 m

Nutritional Information:

Calories	301 kcal
Fat	6.1 g
Carbohydrates	55.7g
Protein	10.8 g
Cholesterol	23 mg
Sodium	1031 mg

* Percent Daily Values are based on a 2,000 calorie diet.

Mozzarella Chicken

Ingredients

- 2 tsps olive oil
- 1 1/2 lbs skinless, boneless chicken parts
- 1 1/2 C. Ranch-style salad dressing
- 2 C. shredded mozzarella cheese

Directions

- Coat a casserole dish with olive oil and then set your oven to 350 degrees before doing anything else.
- Layer your chicken in the dish and top the chicken with ranch.
- Cook the chicken for 25 mins in the oven.
- Then add the cheese and continue cooking it for 14 more mins.

- Enjoy.

Amount per serving (6 total)

Timing Information:

Preparation	10 m
Cooking	35 m
Total Time	45 m

Nutritional Information:

Calories	543 kcal
Fat	45.8 g
Carbohydrates	3.5g
Protein	27.6 g
Cholesterol	103 mg
Sodium	863 mg

* Percent Daily Values are based on a 2,000 calorie diet.

Mexican Beef

Ingredients

- 1/2 tbsp shortening
- 1 1/2 lbs cubed stew meat
- 1 onion, diced
- 1 (14.5 oz.) can stewed tomatoes
- 2 fresh jalapeno chili peppers, seeded and diced
- 2 diced tomatoes
- 1/2 tsp ground cumin
- 1 clove garlic, minced
- salt and pepper to taste
- water as needed

Directions

- Sear your beef in shortening then for 5 mins fry the onions.
- Pour in: canned tomatoes, pepper, jalapenos, garlic, chili peppers, cumin, and fresh tomatoes.

- Get the mix boiling, set the heat to low, and let the contents gently cook, with a lid on the pot, for 50 mins.
- Enjoy.

Amount per serving (4 total)

Timing Information:

Preparation	15 m
Cooking	30 m
Total Time	45 m

Nutritional Information:

Calories	366 kcal
Fat	18 g
Carbohydrates	12g
Protein	38.5 g
Cholesterol	105 mg
Sodium	314 mg

* Percent Daily Values are based on a 2,000 calorie diet.

Mexican Casserole

Ingredients

- 1 1/2 lbs lean ground beef
- 1 (1.25 oz.) package taco seasoning mix
- 1 (16 oz.) can refried beans
- 1 (16 oz.) jar salsa
- 2 C. shredded Monterey Jack cheese

Directions

- Set your oven to 325 degrees before doing anything else.
- Stir fry your beef, remove any excess oils, and add in the taco seasoning.
- Place the contents into a casserole dish and top everything with the salsa, beans, and cheese.
- Cook the casserole in the oven for 27 mins.

- Enjoy.

Amount per serving (8 total)

Timing Information:

Preparation	15 m
Cooking	25 m
Total Time	40 m

Nutritional Information:

Calories	413 kcal
Fat	26.9 g
Carbohydrates	15.4g
Protein	25.9 g
Cholesterol	93 mg
Sodium	1037 mg

* Percent Daily Values are based on a 2,000 calorie diet.

Rancho Minestrone Beef Soup

Ingredients

- 1 lb ground beef
- 1 (10 oz.) can diced tomatoes with green chili peppers
- 1 (16 oz.) can ranch style chili beans
- 1 (15.25 oz.) can whole kernel corn
- 1 (19 oz.) can minestrone soup
- salt and pepper to taste

Directions

- Stir fry your beef, until it is fully, in a big pot.
- Then add in the chili beans, minestrone, diced tomatoes, and corns with juice.

- Add your preferred amount of pepper and salt and place a lid on the pot.
- Cook the stew for 35 mins
- Enjoy.

Amount per serving (4 total)

Timing Information:

Preparation	10 m
Cooking	40 m
Total Time	1 h

Nutritional Information:

Calories	617 kcal
Fat	33.6 g
Carbohydrates	51.9g
Protein	30.3 g
Cholesterol	99 mg
Sodium	1593 mg

* Percent Daily Values are based on a 2,000 calorie diet.

Maggie's Easy Texas Style Black Bean Burgers

(Vegetarian Approved)

Ingredients

- 1 tbsp ground flax seed
- 3 tbsps water
- 1 (15 oz.) can black beans - drained, rinsed, and mashed
- 1/4 C. panko bread crumbs
- 1 clove garlic, minced
- 1/2 tsp salt
- 1/2 tbsp Worcestershire sauce
- 1/8 tsp liquid smoke flavoring
- cooking spray

Directions

- Get a bowl, let the following stand for 10 mins: water and flax seeds.

- Get a 2nd bowl, combine: liquid smoke, flax mix, Worcestershire, beans, salt, panko, and garlic.
- Shape the mix, with your hands, into four burgers.
- Now place everything in the fridge for 1 hour before frying them with nonstick spray for 6 mins each side.
- Enjoy.

Amount per serving (4 total)

Timing Information:

Preparation	10 m
Cooking	10 m
Total Time	55 m

Nutritional Information:

Calories	128 kcal
Fat	1.5 g
Carbohydrates	23.4g
Protein	7.5 g
Cholesterol	0 mg
Sodium	753 mg

* Percent Daily Values are based on a 2,000 calorie diet.

Enchiladas

Ingredients

- 3 (10.75 oz.) cans condensed cream of chicken soup
- 1 pint sour cream
- 1 C. green chili peppers, diced
- 12 (6 inch) corn tortillas
- 1 roasted chicken, shredded
- 8 oz. shredded Colby longhorn cheese
- 8 oz. shredded Muenster cheese
- 2 bunches green onions, diced

Directions

- Set your oven to 375 degrees before doing anything else.
- Get a bowl, combine: green chilies, sour cream, and soup.
- Add an equal amount of the sour cream mix to each tortilla then then some chicken.

- Shape the tortilla into a burrito then place it in a casserole dish.
- Continue for the rest of the ingredients.
- Add a topping of green onions and cheese over everything and cook it all in the oven for 60 mins.
- Enjoy.

Amount per serving (6 total)

Timing Information:

Preparation	10 m
Cooking	1 h
Total Time	1 h 10 m

Nutritional Information:

Calories	975 kcal
Fat	63.6 g
Carbohydrates	46.8g
Protein	55.9 g
Cholesterol	1206 mg
Sodium	1624 mg

* Percent Daily Values are based on a 2,000 calorie diet.

Mexican Style Rice

Ingredients

- 1 (14 oz.) can chicken broth
- 1 (15 oz.) can diced tomatoes with green chili peppers
- 1 tsp salt
- 1 C. brown rice

Directions

- Get the following boiling: rice, broth, salt, and tomatoes.
- Now place a lid on the pot and let the rice gently cook for 60 mins.
- Enjoy.

Amount per serving (4 total)

Timing Information:

Preparation	10 m
Cooking	1 h
Total Time	1 h 10 m

Nutritional Information:

Calories	156 kcal
Fat	1.3 g
Carbohydrates	32.3g
Protein	4 g
Cholesterol	2 mg
Sodium	< 1479 mg

* Percent Daily Values are based on a 2,000 calorie diet.

Cod Stew

Ingredients

- 1/2 onion, diced
- 1 clove garlic, minced
- 1 tbsp chili powder
- 1 1/2 C. chicken broth
- 1 (4 oz.) can canned green chili peppers, diced
- 1 tsp ground cumin
- 1 1/2 C. canned peeled and diced tomatoes
- 1/2 C. diced green bell pepper
- 1/2 C. shrimp
- 1/2 lb cod fillets
- 3/4 C. plain nonfat yogurt

Directions

- Stir fry your onions for 7 mins with some nonstick spray.
- Then combine in the chili powder and the garlic.

- Fry this mix for 4 more mins.
- Now add: cumin, broth, and chili peppers.
- Get everything boiling, set the heat to low, place a lid on the pot, and cook the contents for 22 mins.
- Now add in the cod, tomatoes, shrimp, and bell peppers.
- Get the mix boiling again, place the lid on the pot, set the heat to low, and cook everything for 7 more mins.
- Now begin stirring the mix and add in the yogurt.
- Get the yogurt fully incorporated and shut the heat.
- Enjoy.

Amount per serving (4 total)

Timing Information:

Preparation	10 m
Cooking	30 m
Total Time	40 m

Nutritional Information:

Calories	146 kcal
Fat	1.7 g
Carbohydrates	12.2g
Protein	19.3 g
Cholesterol	46 mg
Sodium	874 mg

* Percent Daily Values are based on a 2,000 calorie diet.

Texas Casserole

Ingredients

- 1 C. water
- 1 C. uncooked instant rice
- 1 lb lean ground beef
- 2 onions, diced
- 1 large green bell pepper, diced
- 1 (14.5 oz.) can diced tomatoes
- 1 (8 oz.) can tomato sauce
- 2 tbsps chili powder
- 1 (8.75 oz.) can whole kernel corn, drained
- salt and pepper to taste
- 3 slices processed American cheese

Directions

- Coat a baking dish with oil and then set your oven to 350 degrees before doing anything else.

- Get 1 C. of water boiling then add the rice.
- Place a lid on the pot and shut the heat.
- Let the contents stand for 10 mins.
- Being to stir fry the green pepper, onions, and beef.
- Get everything hot then add in: chili powder, diced tomatoes, and tomato sauce.
- Now lower the heat and cook the mix for 22 mins.
- Combine the rice into the tomato mix and then add: pepper, salt, and corn.
- Fill your baking dish with the beef mix and top the entire thing with pieces of cheese.
- Cook the casserole in the oven for 23 mins.
- Enjoy.

Amount per serving (6 total)

Timing Information:

Preparation	15 m
Cooking	45 m
Total Time	1 h

Nutritional Information:

Calories	543 kcal
Fat	21.1 g
Carbohydrates	64.5g
Protein	23.8 g
Cholesterol	70 mg
Sodium	720 mg

* Percent Daily Values are based on a 2,000 calorie diet.

Reuben

Ingredients

- 6 skinless, boneless chicken breast halves
- 1/4 tsp salt
- 1/8 tsp ground black pepper
- 1 (16 oz.) can sauerkraut, drained and pressed
- 4 slices Swiss cheese
- 1 1/4 C. thousand island salad dressing
- 1 tbsp diced fresh parsley

Directions

- Coat a baking dish with oil and then set your oven to 325 degrees.
- Layer your chicken in the dish and top it with some pepper and salt.

- Now add the sauerkraut and the cheese.
- Evenly top the contents with the dressing and place a covering of foil around everything.
- Cook the casserole in the oven for 1.5 hrs.
- Before serving the chicken add a garnishing of parsley.
- Enjoy.

Amount per serving (6 total)

Timing Information:

Preparation	5 m
Cooking	1 h 30 m
Total Time	1 h 35 m

Nutritional Information:

Calories	446 kcal
Fat	28.1 g
Carbohydrates	16.7g
Protein	33 g
Cholesterol	104 mg
Sodium	1306 mg

* Percent Daily Values are based on a 2,000 calorie diet.

Texas Mexican Salad

Ingredients

- 1 C. quinoa
- 2 C. water
- 1 tsp kosher salt
- 1/4 C. fresh lime juice
- 2 tbsps olive oil
- 1/8 tsp ground black pepper
- 1 (14 oz.) can diced tomatoes with green chili peppers, drained
- 1 (14 oz.) can garbanzo beans, drained and rinsed
- 1 bunch cilantro, diced
- 2 avocados, cubed
- 1/4 C. crumbled cotija cheese

Directions

- Get your water and quinoa boiling with some salt, place a lid on the pot, and set the heat to low.

- Let the quinoa cook for 27 mins.
- Now get a bowl, combine: garbanzos, lime juice, diced tomatoes, olive oil, and pepper.
- Once the quinoa is done cooking combine in the garbanzo mix.
- Place the lid back on the pot and place everything in the fridge for 3 hrs.
- Add in the cheese, cilantro, and avocados. Then stir the contents before serving.
- Enjoy.

Amount per serving (10 total)

Timing Information:

Preparation	20 m
Cooking	20 m
Total Time	2 h 40 m

Nutritional Information:

Calories	219 kcal
Fat	11.1 g
Carbohydrates	25.7g
Protein	6.3 g
Cholesterol	3 mg
Sodium	515 mg

* Percent Daily Values are based on a 2,000 calorie diet.

A Texas Cajun Egg Sandwich Breakfast

Ingredients

- 1 tbsp butter
- 1 egg
- 1 slice Cheddar cheese
- 1 tsp mayonnaise, or to taste
- 1 tsp mustard, or to taste
- 1 tsp ketchup, or to taste
- 1 pinch Cajun seasoning, or to taste
- 1 dash hot pepper sauce (such as Tabasco(R))
- 2 slices white bread, toasted
- 1 lettuce leaf
- 1 slice tomato

Directions

- Fry your egg for 3 mins in butter then flip it.

- Top the egg with the cheese and cook everything until the cheese melts for about 3 more mins. Then add your Cajun seasoning.
- Coat both your bread pieces with: ketchup, mustard, and mayo.
- Layer a piece of tomato and some lettuce on a piece of bread then put the egg on top and add some hot sauce.
- Add a bit more Cajun spice and add the other piece of bread to from a sandwich.
- Enjoy.

Amount per serving (1 total)

Timing Information:

Preparation	10 m
Cooking	5 m
Total Time	15 m

Nutritional Information:

Calories	471 kcal
Fat	31.5 g
Carbohydrates	29.6g
Protein	18.1 g
Cholesterol	248 mg
Sodium	996 mg

* Percent Daily Values are based on a 2,000 calorie diet.

Easy Texas Grilled Chicken

Ingredients

- 2 tbsps vegetable oil
- 1/4 C. onion, finely diced
- 1 clove garlic, minced
- 3/4 C. ketchup
- 1/3 C. vinegar
- 1 tbsp Worcestershire sauce
- 2 tsps brown sugar
- 1 tsp dry mustard
- 1/2 tsp salt
- 1/4 tsp black pepper
- 1/4 (5 oz.) bottle hot pepper sauce
- 1 (3 lb) chicken, cut into pieces

Directions

- Stir fry your garlic and onions in oil until soft then add: hot sauce, ketchup, pepper, vinegar, salt,

Worcestershire, dry mustard, and brown sugar.
- Get everything boiling, set the heat to a low level, and cook the mix for 12 mins.
- Stir the mix every 3 mins then shut the heat.
- Get your grill hot and coat the grate with oil.
- Grill the chicken for 12 mins per side, until fully done, while coating it regularly with the Worcestershire mix.
- Enjoy.

Amount per serving (6 total)

Timing Information:

Preparation	20 m
Cooking	30 m
Total Time	50 m

Nutritional Information:

Calories	364 kcal
Fat	20.9 g
Carbohydrates	10.6g
Protein	32.4 g
Cholesterol	100 mg
Sodium	679 mg

* Percent Daily Values are based on a 2,000 calorie diet.

Hickory Mushroom Stuffed Burgers

Ingredients

- 5 lbs lean ground beef
- 6 tbsps Worcestershire sauce
- 2 tsps hickory seasoning (optional)
- salt and pepper to taste
- 2 C. diced onion
- 2 C. diced fresh mushrooms
- 2 C. diced cooked ham
- 3 C. shredded Cheddar cheese

Directions

- Get your grill hot and coat the grate with oil.
- Get a bowl, combine: pepper, beef, salt, Worcestershire, and hickory.
- With your hands, form the mix into 20 balls then form the balls

into burgers by pressing down on the balls with a flat surface.
- Lay out your patties and on half of them evenly distribute the following: cheese, onions, ham, and mushrooms.
- Top each patty with another patty which has no toppings and crimp the edges to form a big patty that is stuffed.
- Cook the burgers for 11 mins per side on the grill.
- Enjoy.

Amount per serving (10 total)

Timing Information:

Preparation	15 m
Cooking	15 m
Total Time	30 m

Nutritional Information:

Calories	679 kcal
Fat	47.5 g
Carbohydrates	6.4g
Protein	54 g
Cholesterol	1188 mg
Sodium	1008 mg

* Percent Daily Values are based on a 2,000 calorie diet.

Spicy Sweet Potatoes

Ingredients

- 2 sweet potatoes
- 1 whole jalapeno pepper
- 1/4 C. softened butter
- 1/4 C. orange juice
- 1 tbsp diced fresh cilantro
- sea salt and cracked black pepper to taste
- 2 tbsps melted butter
- 1/4 C. walnut pieces

Directions

- Set your oven to 350 degrees before doing anything else.
- Place your jalapenos on a baking sheet and roast them in the oven for 22 mins. Then remove the skins, dice the peppers, and place them in a bowl.

- At the same time as the peppers are cooking cook the potatoes in the oven cook for 50 mins.
- Once the potatoes are cooked and have cooled off, remove the skins and combine them with the peppers.
- Add the following to the potatoes: cilantro, soft butter, and orange juice.
- Grab a mixer and mix the contents for a few mins until smooth. Then place it all in a casserole dish coated with nonstick spray.
- Top the potatoes with walnuts and melted butter and cook everything in the oven for 23 mins.
- Enjoy.

Amount per serving (4 total)

Timing Information:

Preparation	10 m
Cooking	1 h 5 m
Total Time	1 h 15 m

Nutritional Information:

Calories	307 kcal
Fat	22.3 g
Carbohydrates	25.7g
Protein	3.3 g
Cholesterol	46 mg
Sodium	266 mg

* Percent Daily Values are based on a 2,000 calorie diet.

Maggie's Favorite Armadillo Eggs

Ingredients

- 1 (8 oz.) package cream cheese, softened
- 1/4 C. bacon bits
- 1 tbsp diced fresh chives
- 1 tsp hot sauce
- 1 lb pork sausage
- 1 C. shredded Cheddar cheese
- 1 (5.5 oz.) package seasoned coating mix
- 1/8 tsp ground cumin
- 1/8 tsp chili powder
- 16 fresh jalapeno peppers, butterflied and seeds removed

Directions

- Set your oven to 350 degrees before doing anything else.

- Get a bowl, combine: hot sauce, cream cheese, chives, and bacon bits.
- Get a 2nd bowl, combine: cheddar and sausage.
- Get a 3rd bowl, mix: chili powder, cumin, and coating mix.
- Fill your jalapenos with the cream cheese mix, then cover the peppers with the sausage mix.
- Dip the covered peppers into the dry rub in the 3rd bowl and place everything into a casserole dish that has been coated with nonstick spray.
- Cook everything in the oven for 30 mins.
- Enjoy.

Amount per serving (8 total)

Timing Information:

Preparation	20 m
Cooking	25 m
Total Time	45 m

Nutritional Information:

Calories	397 kcal
Fat	29.5 g
Carbohydrates	16.5g
Protein	17.2 g
Cholesterol	81 mg
Sodium	1227 mg

* Percent Daily Values are based on a 2,000 calorie diet.

Texas Mexican Shark with Noodles

Ingredients

- 1 (16 oz.) package uncooked wide egg noodles
- 1 tsp olive oil
- 1 lb shark steaks, cut into chunks
- 1 lb frozen medium shrimp
- 1 (14.5 oz.) can diced tomatoes and green chilis
- 2 C. shredded mozzarella cheese
- ground black pepper to taste

Directions

- Boil your noodles in salt and water for 9 mins then remove all the liquids.
- Heat the following in olive oil for 2 mins: green chilies, shark meat, tomatoes, and shrimp.

- Place a lid on the pot and cook everything for 17 mins until the shark is fully done and can be flaked.
- Layer your noodles on a serving plate then top the noodles with the shark mix, and then some pepper and mozzarella.
- Enjoy.

Amount per serving (6 total)

Timing Information:

Preparation	15 m
Cooking	23 m
Total Time	40 m

Nutritional Information:

Calories	528 kcal
Fat	14.8 g
Carbohydrates	50.6g
Protein	46.3 g
Cholesterol	232 mg
Sodium	706 mg

* Percent Daily Values are based on a 2,000 calorie diet.

Texas Style Paella

Ingredients

- 2 tbsps olive oil
- 4 chicken leg quarters
- 2 (8 oz.) packages dirty rice mix
- 5 C. water
- 2 lbs whole cooked crawfish, peeled
- 3/4 medium shrimp - peeled and deveined
- 1/2 lb andouille sausage, sliced into rounds
- 2 C. sliced mushrooms
- 1 large green bell pepper, diced
- 1 large sweet onion, diced
- 3 cloves garlic, minced

Directions

- Brown your chicken in oil then add the rice mix and also add the water.

- Get the mix hot and add: garlic, crawfish, onions, shrimp, bell pepper, mushrooms, and sausage.
- Get everything boiling then mix the contents before placing a lid on the pot, setting the heat to low, and cooking the contents for 32 mins.
- Enjoy.

Amount per serving (6 total)

Timing Information:

Preparation	10 m
Cooking	40 m
Total Time	1 h

Nutritional Information:

Calories	757 kcal
Fat	30.5 g
Carbohydrates	62.8g
Protein	54.6 g
Cholesterol	1277 mg
Sodium	1867 mg

* Percent Daily Values are based on a 2,000 calorie diet.

Cajun Fries

Ingredients

- 1/4 C. olive oil
- 1 tsp garlic powder
- 1 tsp onion powder
- 1 tsp chili powder
- 1 tsp Cajun seasoning
- 1 tsp sea salt
- 6 large baking potatoes, sliced into thin wedges

Directions

- Set your oven to 400 degrees before doing anything else.
- Get a big bowl, combine: Cajun spice, olive oil, sea salt, garlic powder, chili powder, and onion powder.
- Place the potatoes into the seasoned oil and toss everything to coat each piece evenly.

- Pour everything into a casserole dish and cook the contents for 40 mins in the oven.
- Now stir the mix with a large spoon and continue cooking for 5 more mins.
- Enjoy.

Amount per serving (6 total)

Timing Information:

Preparation	15 m
Cooking	45 m
Total Time	1 h

Nutritional Information:

Calories	369 kcal
Fat	9.4 g
Carbohydrates	65.5g
Protein	7.7 g
Cholesterol	0 mg
Sodium	399 mg

* Percent Daily Values are based on a 2,000 calorie diet.

Texas Cayenne and Pepper Meatloaf

Ingredients

- 2 bay leaves
- 1 tsp salt
- 1 tsp ground cayenne pepper
- 1 tsp ground black pepper
- 1/2 tsp ground white pepper
- 1/2 tsp ground cumin
- 1/2 tsp ground nutmeg
- 4 tbsps butter
- 3/4 C. diced onion
- 1/2 C. diced green bell pepper
- 1/4 C. diced green onions
- 4 cloves garlic, minced
- 1 tbsp hot pepper sauce
- 1 tbsp Worcestershire sauce
- 1/2 C. evaporated milk
- 1/2 C. ketchup
- 1 1/2 lbs ground beef
- 1/2 lb andouille sausage, casings removed

- 2 eggs, beaten
- 1 C. dried bread crumbs

Directions

- Get a bowl, combine: nutmeg, bay leaves, black and white pepper, salt, cumin, and cayenne.
- Stir fry your onions in butter for 3 mins then add: seasoning mix, bell pepper, Worcestershire, green onions, and hot sauce.
- Cook this mix for 7 mins then add the ketchup and the milk.
- Cook the contents for 3 more mins while mixing.
- Now shut the heat.
- Set your oven to 350 degrees before doing anything else.
- Get a casserole dish and add in your sausage and beef. Then the eggs and the veggie mix.
- Now add in the bread crumbs and mix the contents.

- While mixing take out the bay leaves then shape the meat into a loaf.
- Cook the loaf for 26 mins then set the oven to 400 degrees and cook it for 36 more mins.
- Enjoy.

Amount per serving (8 total)

Timing Information:

Preparation	20 m
Cooking	1 h
Total Time	1 h 20 m

Nutritional Information:

Calories	548 kcal
Fat	40.8 g
Carbohydrates	19.3g
Protein	25.7 g
Cholesterol	158 mg
Sodium	1184 mg

* Percent Daily Values are based on a 2,000 calorie diet.

Southern Linguine

Ingredients

- 4 oz. linguine pasta
- 2 skinless, boneless chicken breast halves
- 2 tsps Cajun seasoning
- 2 tbsps butter
- 1 red bell pepper, sliced
- 1 green bell pepper, sliced
- 4 fresh mushrooms, sliced
- 1 green onion, diced
- 1 C. heavy cream
- 1/4 tsp dried basil
- 1/4 tsp lemon pepper
- 1/4 tsp salt
- 1/8 tsp garlic powder
- 1/8 tsp ground black pepper
- 1/4 C. grated Parmesan cheese

Directions

- Cook your pasta in water and salt for 9 mins, then remove all the liquids.
- Coat your pieces of chicken with the Cajun seasoning then stir fry them in butter for 8 mins.
- Now add in: green onions, bell peppers, garlic powder, and salt.
- Fry this mix for 5 more mins before lowering the heat and combining in: black pepper, cream, more garlic powder, lemon pepper, and salt.
- Get the contents hot, then add the pasta and stir everything.
- Top the Cajun pasta with some parmesan before serving.
- Enjoy.

Amount per serving (2 total)

Timing Information:

Preparation	20 m
Cooking	20 m
Total Time	40 m

Nutritional Information:

Calories	935 kcal
Fat	61.7 g
Carbohydrates	54g
Protein	43.7 g
Cholesterol	271 mg
Sodium	1189 mg

* Percent Daily Values are based on a 2,000 calorie diet.

Texas Style Spicy Rice

Ingredients

- 1 lb lean ground beef
- 1 lb beef sausage
- 1 onion, finely diced
- 1 (8 oz.) package dirty rice mix
- 2 C. water
- 1 (10 oz.) can diced tomatoes with green chili peppers
- 2 (15 oz.) cans kidney beans, drained
- salt and pepper to taste

Directions

- Fry your beef, onions, and sausage.
- Then remove the excess oils.
- Now get the following boiling: chilies, rice mix, diced tomatoes, and 2 C. of water.

- Add in the beans, pepper, and salt.
- Get the mix boiling again then add the onion mix. Bring everything to a boil and place a lid on the pot.
- Let the contents cook for 30 mins with a low level of heat.
- Enjoy.

Amount per serving (8 total)

Timing Information:

Preparation	15 m
Cooking	35 m
Total Time	50 m

Nutritional Information:

Calories	485 kcal
Fat	23.5 g
Carbohydrates	41.4g
Protein	26.2 g
Cholesterol	72 mg
Sodium	1541 mg

* Percent Daily Values are based on a 2,000 calorie diet.

Thanks for Reading! Now Let's Try some Sushi and Dump Dinners....

Send the Book!

To grab this **box set** simply follow the link mentioned above, or tap the book cover.

This will take you to a page where you can simply enter your email address and a PDF version of the **box set** will be emailed to you.

I hope you are ready for some serious cooking!

[Send the Book!](#)

You will also receive updates about all my new books when they are free.

Also don't forget to like and subscribe on the social networks. I love meeting my readers. Links to all my profiles are below so please click and connect :)

[Facebook](#)

[Twitter](#)

COME ON...
LET'S BE FRIENDS :)

I adore my readers and love connecting with them socially. Please follow the links below so we can connect on Facebook, Twitter, and Google+.

[Facebook](#)

[Twitter](#)

I also have a blog that I regularly update for my readers so check it out below.

[My Blog](#)

Can I Ask A Favour?

If you found this book interesting, or have otherwise found any benefit in it. Then may I ask that you post a review of it on Amazon? Nothing excites me more than new reviews, especially reviews which suggest new topics for writing. I do read all reviews and I always factor feedback into my newer works.

So if you are willing to take ten minutes to write what you sincerely thought about this book then please visit our Amazon page and post your opinions.

Again thank you!

Interested in Other Easy Cookbooks?

Everything is easy! Check out my Amazon Author page for more great cookbooks:

For a complete listing of all my books please see my author page.

Made in the USA
Coppell, TX
05 January 2025

44008112R00098